Coach Yourself Through Grief

Coach Yourself Through Grief

Dr. Don Eisenhauer, PCC

Dr. Don Eisenhauer, PCC

Email: don@coachingatendoflife.com

Phone: 1-484-948-1894

Web site: www.coachingatendoflife.com

Coaching at End of Life

Copyright © 2014 Coaching at End of Life, LLC, Dr. Don Eisenhauer. All rights reserved. No part of this publication shall be reproduced or transmitted in any form or by any electronic, mechanical, photocopying or recording means, or otherwise, including information storage and retrieval systems, without permission in writing from the copyright holder.

ISBN 978-0-9894751-1-2

Table of Contents

Acknowledgments vii

Introduction 1

Chapter One: "Through Grief" 3

Chapter Two: "Coach Yourself" 5

Chapter Three: Grief Coaching Principles 15

Chapter Four: Dealing with the Losses of Life 51

Chapter Five: Our Culture's View of Grief 63

Chapter Six: The Church: Help or Hindrance?................. 65

Chapter Seven: Finding an End-of-Life Coach 75

Chapter Eight: Grief Support Groups................................. 77

Chapter Nine: Anytime Grief Support............................... 81

Chapter Ten: How Do I Become an End-of-Life Coach?... 83

Resources:

    Principles for Coaching Yourself Through Grief 87

    Download the Coaching at End of Life App 89

    Free eBook: Life Lessons from Dragonflies 91

References 87

About the Author 89

Acknowledgments

In memory of my father, Russell S. Eisenhauer

1928 – 2004

Dad taught me what it means to die well ... then I learned what it is like to experience grief.

This book evolved as a result of my grief journey and the support of those who walked with me. These are principles that I have taught professionally for years and have come to understand personally.

I miss you Dad. I am grateful for all that you taught me— through your life and through your death.

Introduction

Rarely a day goes by that I do not receive a phone call from someone I have never met who says, "My (loved one) has just died, and I am not doing well. Can you help me?"

Grief is an experience that most of us will be forced to deal with at one time or another. It is not something we choose. Yet, it is a part of life.

Some people will call out for help, as I described above. Most, however, will walk the journey of grief on their own, hoping someone will support them along the way.

The problem is that few individuals rush to support those in grief. Most turn the other way. The one in grief generally walks alone as friends and family react out of their own ignorance or fear. That saddens me.

This is why, at Coaching at End of Life, we have committed to "boldly go where most don't want, but someday, all will," as our Star Trek-inspired tagline reads.

We are committed to training and raising up certified end-of-life coaches, who will be available to walk the journey of grief with those who have experienced loss. Most of us need that support. We need that companionship. We need that affirmation and that listening ear. As the calls continue to come in to my desk, I respond by saying, "Yes! We can help you. Let me direct you to an end-of-life coach who would love to walk your journey with you."

Even if you have an end-of-life coach, he can't walk with you 24/7. There are times when you wake up in the middle of the night, overwhelmed by your grief. There are times when you must take steps on your own.

That is the purpose of this book. It is meant to be placed into the hands of those who are experiencing grief. You are not alone. At Coaching at End of Life, we want to walk with you.

Allow me to share how you can coach yourself through grief.

Chapter One
"Through Grief"

There are four words that make up the title of this book. Very little needs to be said about the last two words. As part of life, most people will experience what it means to go "through grief." The very fact that you picked up this book says that you are probably experiencing grief right now. If not right now, you might have had a loved one die in the past and are still feeling the effects of that loss today. (For some, that loss was so long ago, you are embarrassed to outwardly admit that you still hurt. You might be reading this book in secret.) Others are reading this book because grief is something you anticipate in the near future—someone you love is dying, or is getting older, or has been diagnosed with a terminal illness. I commend you for wanting to "prepare" yourself.

Very few of us escape going "through grief." When we experience a loss—when someone we love dies—we understand what many describe as a pain so severe that it cannot be put into words. Clients and members of my grief support groups say to me, "I never imagined that grief would hurt so much," or "I had no clue how difficult this would be."

That word "through" is important. I sometimes compare the journey of grief to a tunnel. Tunnels are not fun places. They are dark and scary. Many choose to avoid them. But the only way to get to the other side is to go through. (Eisenhauer, *Coaching at End of Life*, 2012, p. 35.)

How do we do that? Most of us never took a class on "how to walk through grief." Above, I commended those of you who are reading this book as a way to prepare yourself for an impending loss. You are rare. Very few prepare for grief ahead of time. Most do their learning while they are in the midst of it. And that is not easy to do.

So how do we walk through grief? The answer can be found in the first two words of this book's title.

Chapter Two
"Coach Yourself"

The first two words of this book's title need a little more explanation. When you hear the word "coach," what image comes to mind? Some think of a carriage—a two- or four-wheeled vehicle (often horse-drawn) used to transport people. The image that comes to mind for some women is a designer handbag. The most common image when people hear the word "coach" is the leader of a sports team. This image will be helpful in understanding the first two words of the title of this book, and how a "coach" can help us walk through our grief.

What do we know about a football coach?

- **Having a coach is a necessity for a football team.** It would be difficult for a team to play a game without a coach. In the same way, it is just as difficult to think about walking the journey of grief without a coach. Whether it is a certified end-of-life coach listed on the coachingatendoflife.com website, or a pastor/chaplain/spiritual leader, or a relative or friend, it is never easy and usually not advisable to walk through grief alone.

Coach Yourself Through Grief

[Allow me to part from the football coach analogy for a moment to define the title used above—"certified end-of-life coach." You might think to yourself, "I don't need an end-of-life coach. My loved one has already died." Perhaps the analogy to use here is the coin toss at the beginning of a football game. There is one coin that is thrown up into the air, but there are two sides to that coin. Players choose either "heads" or "tails." In a similar way, there are two sides to the one coin called "end of life." There is the time leading up to death, which we call the process of dying. For the loved ones of the deceased, there is also the time period following the death, which we call grief. Most people find it helpful to have someone walk with them through both of these time periods. An end-of-life coach is one who helps people who are dying (as well as their families) and those who are grieving. A certified end-of-life coach is one who has been trained and certified by Coaching at End of Life. He/she is qualified to coach those on both sides of the end-of-life coin.]

- **A football coach does not join his players on the field nor does he play the game for them.** He stays on the sideline. In a similar way, an end-of-life coach doesn't do your mourning for you. Her "job description" is to walk alongside of you, giving you the support you need as YOU do the hard work of grief.

- **The coach's role is to bring out the best in his players and to motivate them to work hard, no matter how difficult it gets.** In the same way, your end-of-life coach is your cheerleader who encourages you to keep

Chapter Two: "Coach Yourself"

working and to keep mourning. The mourning process is often the most difficult thing anyone has to face. It is common to want to give up. Your end-of-life coach is there by your side, encouraging you to keep moving forward.

This is what it means to be "coached" through grief. Clearly the coach is invaluable to a football team and to an individual who is grieving. But what if you don't have a coach? Or even if you do, what about those times when your coach is not available? What happens when you wake up in the middle of the night and you are alone? What do you do when you hear a song that was a favorite of your loved one, and you break down and cry? Where can you find support when you try to share your pain by calling out to family members and friends, and they put you down because you aren't over it yet? How about the times between sessions with your coach, when you want to move forward on your own? What do you do when you feel like giving up, and it's not a time when your end-of-life coach is physically by your side? That is where the second word of this book title comes into play. This is when you need to coach yourself through your grief.

How do you do that?

Remind yourself what your end-of-life coach would say to you, if you had one.

How do you know what she would say? It is in the contents of this book, especially the next chapter. Chapter Three will teach you eight things you can do that will help you during the tough times of walking through your grief. These are coaching principles you might need to apply to yourself repeatedly. (Note the subtitle of this book—Applying Coaching Principles to Your Grief Journey.) These are action steps that you will put into practice over and over again.

Remind yourself what it means to be grieving well.

Misunderstandings abound in end-of-life issues. Allow me to share one of them that will affect your ability to coach yourself through grief.

It is important to ask the following question. When I am in the midst of grief, what does it mean that "I am doing well"?

Because we live in a culture that acts like death is optional rather than inescapable, we typically don't learn how to grieve a loss. As a result, I will often hear a person grieving a recent death say something like, "I am doing well now. I have a smile on my face and I am feeling good. Last week, however, I was not doing well at all. I lost it. I was crying and hurt so much I could barely function." This person has it totally backwards. It is "now" that I would question how well he is doing. Last week is when he was truly "doing well"!

Our culture and the church do not get this. It is the opposite of the way we typically think. In reality, crying or outwardly mourning a loss is often a sign of doing well. Holding it all together or keeping the feelings pressed down inside is often a sign of unhealthy grief. In order to coach ourselves through grief, we must understand this.

Chapter Two: "Coach Yourself"

Coaching yourself through grief includes reminding yourself that what you are experiencing is not merely okay; it is good. It is what you need to experience in order to work through your grief. It is all part of the process of mourning a loss.

Shield yourself from the many myths that surround the topic of grief.

Myths are false ideas that are regularly presented as truth. If you don't guard yourself against them, it becomes easy to get sucked into accepting these myths as reality.

Ten common myths of grief are:

Myth #1: Grief and mourning are the same experience.

Grief is what one feels on the inside after a loved one has died—sadness, loneliness, anger, guilt, etc. It includes both thoughts and feelings about our loss. Mourning is the outward expression of that grief. It is the external and visible expression of what is experienced on the inside. Some examples of mourning include crying, talking about the deceased person, funeral or memorial services, acknowledging anniversary dates, the lighting of candles, etc. It is not enough for a person to feel her grief. Healthy grief must involve mourning.

Myth #2: The grief process is orderly and predictable.

Dr. Elizabeth Kubler-Ross, in her groundbreaking book *On Death and Dying* (1973), laid out for us the stages of grief—denial, anger, bargaining, depression, and acceptance. The myth is that every grief experience will follow this orderly progression, from stage one to stage five. That is not what Dr. Kubler-Ross was trying to express! Although these stages are real, everyone grieves in his own unique way, and it is most frequently an uneven process. There are many factors that affect our mourning—our relationship with the person who died, the circumstances surrounding the death, age, culture, faith, etc.

Myth #3: The best thing one can do is to keep busy and avoid the pain of grief.

We learn that pain is an indication that something is wrong and that we should find ways to alleviate the pain. In grief, the opposite is true. The best thing one can do in grief is to open oneself to the presence of one's pain. Crazy as it sounds, a grieving person's pain is the key that opens his heart and moves him forward on his way to healing. Staying busy may be helpful in short-term coping by masking the pain; however, it merely postpones one's grieving.

Myth #4: The goal of mourning is to "get over it."

As I work with the grieving, I frequently hear variations of these questions: "Am I over it yet?" or "When will I ever get over this?" Even worse are the comments of others, "They should be over it by now and get on with life!" Even though other people want the mourner to get over his grief because it will make him feel better, it is not going to happen. Rather, the one grieving will learn to move forward and enjoy life again, in spite of the pain of loss that will always be there.

Myth #5: Tears and other displays of emotion are a sign of weakness.

Crying is a wonderful way to mourn a loss—to release the pain inside. This is true for both women and men, and in no way shows a sign of weakness. Quite the contrary, it takes a strong man to face his emotions and to let them out through his tears. Look at the way that God regards your emotions. Psalm 56:8 (CEV) says, "You have stored my tears in your bottle and counted each of them." The Lord God, ruler of the universe, tenderly collects the tears you shed. He saves them all and records each of them in His eternal record. That is how important your emotions are!

Myth #6: Grief is only an emotional reaction.

Grief affects a person in far more ways than emotionally. A few examples of the different responses to the experience of grief are hyper- or hypoactivity, insomnia or sleeping all the time, and uncontrolled appetite or having no appetite at all. "I never knew grief would be this painful" is a comment I hear regularly.

Myth #7: Nobody can help you with your grief.

The truth is that those in the midst of grief need other people — supportive people who understand the process of grief. This is why end-of-life coaches are so much in need. Many find this help in grief support groups as well. (See Chapter Eight.)

Myth #8: Time heals all wounds.

Although this old cliché is stated often, the truth is that time alone has nothing to do with healing. To heal, one must mourn and walk through the grief journey. It is true that this journey takes time, but unless one does the work of mourning, time itself will accomplish nothing but to prolong the grief.

Myth #9: Moving on with your life means you're forgetting the one you lost.

We never get over our grief, but we can reconcile it and move forward with a meaningful life. This can serve to honor our loved one. We will continue to remember them as we discover our "new normal."

Myth #10: Grief finally ends.

This myth says that when we do all the right things, and grief and mourning are finally reconciled, they will never come up again. This is not true. Even many years following a death, deep bursts of grief pain are common.

I recently visited one of my hospice patients, who was typically a cheery person. This particular day when I walked in, she was crying hysterically. I asked what had happened. She said, "I miss my mom." She had just attended a special service at the facility where she lives. It brought back memories of her mom. I asked when her mom died, and she told me her mom died in a plague when my patient was six years old. My patient is currently 97 years old. Her mother died 91 years ago, and on this day she was crying hysterically because she missed her. This is perfectly normal, healthy grief. My patient was doing well!

Ask yourself questions that cause deep, personal introspection.

It doesn't have to be in times of crises that you coach yourself through grief. Coaching yourself can be an intentional, helpful practice you choose to further your progress. It is a time of reflection and honest self-examination—asking yourself where you are in your grief; evaluating how you are responding to the loss you have experienced; thinking about where you want to be and what it will take to get

Chapter Two: "Coach Yourself"

there; and considering what the "new normal" might look like.

For example, in the next chapter, you will read about the importance of finding safe people and safe places, where you can honestly express whatever you are feeling and experiencing. Coaching yourself would mean that, while reading that chapter, you would ask yourself questions like: Do I have those safe people and those safe places where I can share honestly? What are the emotions I am feeling? What, in my journey of grief, have I experienced today? Who can I tell about my experience, and how would doing that be a help to me? What are the emotions or experiences that I have been afraid to share with anyone? Questions such as these will arise when reading this book. If they don't, I suggest that you pause in your reading of each section or chapter and ask yourself similar questions. Ask yourself how you are doing with each of the principles.

Identify some realistic, forward-moving action steps—"My next step in finding safe people and safe places is that I must …" or "I am going to do that on …"

You might want to write these down and discuss them later with your end-of-life coach. This also includes identifying areas of growth and learning that have come as a result of this unwanted grief journey.

Take the responsibility to find other available resources.

Chapters Eight and Nine talk about getting connected with a grief support group—either in person, over the telephone, or via the internet. You will also learn about the anytime grief support, where you can go to the coachingatendoflife.com website 24/7 to find support.

Chapter Three
Grief Coaching Principles

If you had a certified end-of-life coach, what would happen if you sat down with her right now? First, she would listen to your story. She would NOT step in and do your mourning for you. She would stay on the sidelines. But, she would walk your journey with you and would assist you in applying the following action steps to your life.

In coaching yourself through grief, you will apply these same principles to yourself.

1. Find a Safe Place

Because of the culture in which we live, most people do not understand the journey of grief. The one who grieves may act according to how he feels today, but most bystanders don't know how to respond. Because THEY are uncomfortable, they push the grieving person to "get over it." The result is a society filled with grieving people who feel misunderstood or alone in their grief. Because many have found disapproval for their method of grieving, they have learned to keep to themselves and not share with anyone. "It's just not safe," they say.

Grief produces a wide range of normal emotions. Some of the typical emotions of grief are shock, sadness, anxiety, guilt, hopelessness, fear, disorganization, confusion, anger, hatred, jealousy, joy, and relief, just to name a few. These emotions are not always the easiest to handle.

The picture below is what H. Norman Wright calls the "Tangled Ball of Emotions." It shows what the emotions of grief are like for many people. They are all tangled and mixed together, at times making it difficult to sort out the emotions being experienced. The emotions are unpredictable—the griever can feel fine one moment and then, all of a sudden, be crying uncontrollably. Sometimes the emotions feel overwhelming and sometimes out of control.

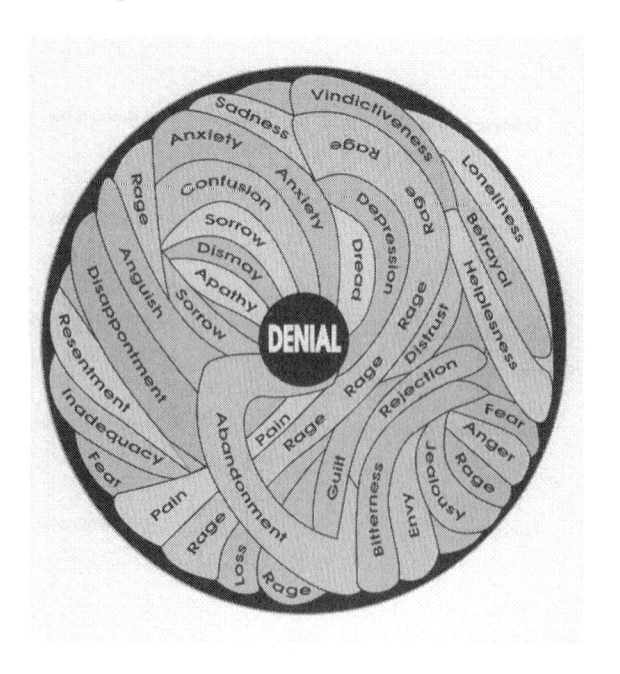

Reprinted with permission. (Wright, *Helping Those Who Hurt*, 2006, 64)

Chapter Three: Grief Coaching Principles

Right in the center of this circle is denial. This is the initial emotion that most individuals experience when they hear the news of the death of a loved one. They feel shock, numbness, and disbelief. There is the feeling of being dazed or stunned. I believe these feelings are gifts from God. They psychologically protect those who learn of a loved one's death, until they are able to tolerate what they don't want to believe. They are a temporary time-out, until they are able to face the full reality of the death. I sometimes describe denial as a "natural injection of anesthesia." Especially in the beginning of the grief journey, one's emotions need time to catch up with what the mind has been told. I believe that if we were hit with all the feelings of grief at one time, we would not be able to survive them. Then, after the initial denial, one by one we can face all the emotions above and accept the reality of the death. That's when the hard work of grieving begins and where the emotions can easily get out of control.

It is easy to see why many are uncomfortable with someone who is grieving. It is understandable that family and friends will try to get their loved ones "over" their grief, and to stop the grievers when they openly express these emotions. But it is equally clear and understandable that, as a result, those in the midst of grief do not feel safe in sharing with many people.

Hence, when you are the one in grief, one of the first action steps you must take is to find a safe place where you can openly mourn your loss in your own way. You must find "safe" people with whom you can share, and "safe" groups and organizations who will give you permission to be yourself.

What do you look for in finding "safe" people or groups?

Before I answer that question in the sections below, let me begin with this caveat: Although all of the grief reactions below are normal and expected, if you continue to experience them over an extended period of time without change, or if you find yourself wanting to harm yourself or others, you should seek immediate help from a mental health professional.

Find Someone Who Will Allow You to Hurt

One of the most difficult tasks in the grief process is to allow yourself to hurt. It is also one of the most difficult tasks of a "safe" person who desires to walk the journey of grief with you. The reality is clear—grief hurts. The normal tendency when someone hurts is to want to feel better. Likewise, the normal tendency of your friends and family will be to help you feel better. You will want to find someone who will refrain from this. As a matter of fact, you will want to find someone who is comfortable with your pain. It was stated earlier that loss has to be grieved and mourned; the pain needs to be faced head on. The only way to move beyond the feelings of grief is to walk through them. You want to find a "safe" person who will sit with you in your pain, not try to remove your pain. He will walk the journey of suffering with you, not tell you to be strong, or to buck it up, or to keep busy. If he gives in to the natural instinct to try to remove your hurt, he may remove the opportunity for real healing to occur. In addition, he may subconsciously send you the message that hurting is wrong and that, if you are going to hurt, being around him is not a safe place to do so.

Find Someone Who Will Allow You to Cry

On the heels of "find someone who will allow you to hurt" is "find someone who will allow you to cry." We already stated that crying is a good, healthy outlet for our pain. Crying is a form of mourning. (Again, the natural instinct of friends and family is to help the crier feel better. They rush over to give a hug. They hand out tissues. There are times when these gestures are appreciated by you in your grief. Sometimes, however, the message is, "Wipe those tears. It's time to stop crying." That is not the type of person you want to be around!) You want to find a "safe" person who somehow conveys, "I love your tears. Go ahead and cry if you want." And when you have stopped crying and are again able to speak, you want someone around you who will say something like, "Tell me about the tears…" This is a "safe" individual!

Find Someone Who Will Give You Permission to Feel Whatever You Feel

A safe place is a place where you can feel whatever you feel without being told that you shouldn't feel that way, or that you need to get over it or deal with it, or that what you are feeling is not a very godly feeling, or that you need to stop because you are not being a good testimony to others. These are comments I hear spoken all the time. The result is always the same. You learn that "this is not a safe place where I can be real."

Coach Yourself Through Grief

When you are grieving, you feel some intense emotions. You need a safe place to get those emotions out. The anger you might feel (which is your form of protest by saying "This is not what I wanted to happen!") might be directed toward a doctor, toward your loved one, toward God, or even toward other friends or family.

I was the end-of-life coach for a man who was dying. Prior to his death, I met with this man in the afternoon. His wife told me, "You need to tell John that he must get better. You must pray that God will spare him. I am not ready to lose my husband." Later that evening I received news that John had died, and I was asked to come to the house. When I arrived, the wife ran toward me and literally started punching me, while yelling, "You didn't do your job. You were supposed to tell him to stay alive." She wasn't really angry with me, but there was a lot of anger inside that needed to be let out. I was that safe place where she could do so. In the months to come, I was able to walk the journey of grief with her, and she felt safe and able to be herself.

Below are a few things to remember about emotions, especially as they relate to grief:

- You are not your emotions. Your emotions and feelings come and go.
- Feelings aren't good or bad, they just are.
- It's okay to feel sad and cry. Jesus cried when His friend died (John 11:35).
- It's okay to feel anger. Many of the prophets of the Bible, and even Jesus, felt angry.

Chapter Three: Grief Coaching Principles

- It's okay to feel happy, laugh, and have fun. You can't be sad all the time, and sometimes you just need to get your mind off the work of grieving and have fun with friends.

- It's okay to feel guilty. You may have had a fight with the person who died or wished that person dead. Your wishing cannot kill anybody. Maybe you wished you had spent more time with the person or had done what she asked you to do. If you are having a hard time with feelings of this kind, talk to your coach, or try writing a letter to the person who died.

- It's okay to feel afraid. You may be afraid because you're not sure who will take care of you, where the money will come from, or how you'll survive without the one you love. Sit down with your coach or a trusted adult and discuss your concerns.

- It's okay to feel these feelings in your body. God built our bodies to handle stress.

- You may find that you actually feel relieved if a death ends a long illness or other difficult situation. This feeling can be hard to admit, but it's normal.

- It's okay to feel disorganized or panicked. You may even experience anxiety attacks. These usually pass, but they are uncomfortable.

- It's okay to not feel anything. You may go out with friends, laugh, and have fun after you hear about a death. It's one way your emotional self protects itself from a big shock.

Find Someone Who Will Give You Permission to Say Whatever You Want to Say

Because of the intense emotions, grieving people sometimes say things that would not normally be acceptable things to say. You might verbalize extreme anger toward other individuals or toward God. In normal situations, a person like this might be asked to "watch his mouth" or "not speak that way." When you are in grief following the loss of a loved one, however, you want to find someone who will listen intently as you talk, encouraging you to share more. This will enable you to release what you are feeling. In this situation, it is not only acceptable, it is healthy.

When in grief, you might say that you have no hope to go on, that life is now without meaning, or that you wish your life was over. (In a normal situation, the person who says something like this needs to be placed on a suicide watch with professional help. Most grieving people who say these words, however, have no intention of killing themselves. They are simply saying, "This is how much I hurt," and "This is how much I am going to miss my loved one." They still need to be questioned to make sure they have no plans to harm themselves. Talk of suicide always needs to be taken seriously.) What you need more than anything, however, is to know that you're in a safe environment where you can share even this deepest feeling and pain. You want to find someone who will respond to you by saying something like, "It sounds like you are really hurting. Tell me more about the pain you are feeling," or "To actually bring harm to yourself is not acceptable behavior. But it sure makes sense that you hurt enough to say such things. Share with me more of what is going on with you now."

In your grief, you do not need someone to correct the things you are saying, nor do you need someone to try to change your thinking to be more positive. You need a person who will sit with you and allow you to say whatever you need to say as you process the many emotions you are experiencing.

There are times when you might not want to say anything. Don't let anyone press you to do so. Remember that you are in charge. Find someone who will be comfortable to sit with you in silence. Someone who gives you times of silence might be giving you the greatest gifts anyone could give. Mourning requires periods of silence and solitude. Many who don't understand the grief journey (or who want to step in and fix you) will not allow this silence. The mystery of grief is such that words are often inadequate. Silence helps to create a safe place for you in your grief.

Find Someone Who Gives You Permission to Do Whatever You Want to Do

Keeping in mind the caveat regarding professional help from a mental health expert where appropriate, the next step in this progression is to find someone who will permit you to do whatever you want.

A long-time member of my church recently died. His wife, Mary, a devout Christian, was grieving appropriately. She was crying and mourning her loss. She was lonely and missed her husband terribly. A few weeks into her grief, some of her friends came to me, worried about Mary. Mary told them she didn't want to come to church anymore. She hurt too badly and just wanted to stay home. I asked what they told her. The friends told Mary she needed to be in church, and she needed to be surrounded by other people. But things only got worse for Mary, and she threatened all the more to stay home. The friends asked me to talk to her and to convince her she must continue to attend church. I told them I would talk to her, but that I was going to give her permission to stay home and that they needed to give her the same permission. Mary stayed home for two Sundays and then returned, saying church is where she wanted to be. But Mary needed to figure that out for herself. The only way she could do that was to have the freedom to stay home.

Some will clean out their loved one's clothes right away, while others will wait a long time to do so. Neither way is "right"! Some will attend a support group, while others will spend long periods of time alone. Some will visit their doctor to get medication to help them face their grief, while others will refuse any form of medication. As long as you are doing your work of mourning, you need to grieve in your own way and do whatever you want. The person who allows you to choose your own path, supporting you where you are, will provide a "safe" place for you.

Find Someone Who Will Not Try to Fix You

I have said this all along, but I will say it again. When you are in the midst of grief, you do not need to be fixed. The more you are mourning and letting out your grief, especially initially, the better you are doing. What you do need, however, is a coach to walk the journey with you. But

Chapter Three: Grief Coaching Principles

in order for your coach to be able to make a difference, he has to establish a "safe" place for you, where you can be real and can face your grief head on.

2. Board the Roller Coaster and Hold on Tight

The second action step is for you to board the roller coaster and hold on tight.

I know no better picture to describe the journey of grief than a roller coaster. There are times of being at great heights, followed by steep drops of emotions to the very bottom. The ups and downs continue, often at unexpected intervals. At the same time, grief does not follow a direct route. There are twists and turns, and times when life turns completely upside down. It comes to a sudden stop, then starts all over again. Thus describes the journey of grief.

After giving yourself permission to ride the roller coaster, what most of you need is someone to ride the roller coaster with you. This is the "safe" person we described in action step 1. Most of us don't need someone to tell us when to get on or off. We don't need someone to give riding instructions. We don't need correction as to how to ride better; we simply need a companion along the journey.

This was driven home to me in my early years of pastoral ministry. Some members of my congregation died. I ministered to these families and offered what I thought were some great, insightful instructions to help them deal with their grief. (I now realize that I probably greatly annoyed them.) Then I received a call that the child of a family was dead. I went to the house and sat with the family for hours. I was so distraught by what happened that I didn't know what to say. I gave no instructions. I offered no advice. I simply sat with the family in silence, crying with them. After many hours, I got up and left. I felt like the worst, most ineffective pastor in the world. I thought I had been totally useless to this family. Yet in the days to come, I was told over and over what an incredible help I had been. They could not thank me enough for ministering to them so effectively. I thought, "What???? I did nothing but sit there with them." That was exactly what they needed. They didn't need my wise words of instruction. They needed me to be present. They needed me to ride the roller coaster with them. And that is exactly what most of us need.

Expected and Unexpected Friends

It is often surprising for the one in grief to see who will ride the roller coaster with them and who will not. Often those whom they expect to board the coaster with them are never seen again. Some whom they thought would never be present become their closest companions.

I share this because the expected and unexpected friend issue often becomes one that is heavy on the heart of the grieving. It hurts when you expect your close, longtime friend to be there for you and to allow you to share whatever you are experiencing, and she is not. It comes as a surprise and makes no sense. The inability of expected friends to be present can be a secondary grief issue, and something that needs to be grieved and worked through. Don't beat yourself up for feeling this way. It is a common feeling of many in grief. Let that feeling out.

Embrace Your Feelings

One of the reasons many friends or family stay clear of you when you are riding the roller coaster is because they don't know how to handle you. They don't know what to do with you. Often they will try to make you better. (They reason that if they can make you feel better, then they will feel better. They won't be so uncomfortable around you!) But that is not what you need. What will help you best is to embrace the feelings you are experiencing. Become a friend with these emotions—not a life-long friend, but a friend for the near future.

What I just described is the opposite of how we typically deal with painful feelings. If I accidentally touch a hot stove with my hand, I quickly move my hand away. I remove any and all possible painful feelings. In this case, what is typically best is to allow yourself to experience the full brunt of these emotions.

In Chapter Two, I explored 10 of the common myths regarding grief. Do you remember the first myth? "Grief and mourning are the same experience." Grief is what one feels on the inside after a loved one has died. It is all the internal thoughts and feelings about loss. Mourning is the outward expression of that grief. It is the external and visible expression of what is experienced on the inside.

If we don't become a temporary friend with those feelings, experience them, and let them out through mourning, they will find their own way to come out. And when those feelings of grief come out on their own, it is not pretty. They come out as explosive anger, depression, physical illness, or as risky or immoral behavior.

So when a loved one dies and you see the line for the roller coaster forming, don't turn around and run the other way. Board the roller coaster and hold on tight.

3. Tell Your Story

The third action step is to tell your story. One of the most helpful things we can do is to tell our story. It's part of the way we let our grief out. Most of us in grief love to tell our story. It's part of the process of mourning on the path toward healing. It is a way we acknowledge the reality of our loss. It allows us to recognize and admit our emotions and pain. It's an important way that we look back in order to remember and to hold onto memories. It's a wonderful step in our process of looking forward in the hope of discovering renewed meaning and purpose.

What makes telling our story difficult is that there are not many people who will give us that opportunity. Telling our story takes time. In our fast-paced society, many don't want to give up that time. Telling our story takes a "safe" person with a receptive spirit. We already discussed how difficult it is to find those individuals. In telling our story, we sometimes go on and on about the minute details of our loved one's sickness or death. We sometimes share far more than our listeners ever wanted to hear. That's what we need to do. That is normal in grief. But you should know that many will get frustrated with you. The hearing of our story takes patience on their part—patience they may not have.

Chapter Three: Grief Coaching Principles

We might even find ourselves sharing the same story over and over again. Each time we tell it, it is as if it is brand new. Repeating the story is a way of processing and accepting the death. Again, as a reality check, not everyone has the patience to listen to our same story over and over, and that will be obvious. This greatly affects our grieving process and blocks our progress toward healing.

Who is the "safe" individual who is willing to listen to you? It might be a relative. It might be a friend. It might be a pastor. It might be a member of your church. It might be someone who attends the same grief support group. You can always log on to the coachingatendoflife.com website and hire a certified end-of-life coach. Listening to your story is exactly what they are trained to do. It really doesn't matter who it is, but in order to move forward in your grief journey, your story must be told.

What will be included in your stories?

Memories

One of the things you will likely include in your story is memories of times spent with your loved one. Aren't you thinking of those memories constantly? Most of us in grief have an endless supply of memories ready to share!

The memories we have are precious gifts from God which no one can take away. They are ours to hold onto forever. We keep our loved one alive by sharing them.

Relationship

Most of us will also include in our stories detailed information about the relationship we shared with our loved one who died. We include strengths about our relationship, as well as things we wish had been different. This is our attempt to work through our feelings of guilt and regret, to come to our own conclusion that we had done our best, or to grant ourselves forgiveness if we have failed. All of that is accomplished in the sharing of our story. The only way many of us can come to peace within ourselves is if we come to our own resolution about these issues. Therefore, we do not need our "safe" individuals to comment on our relationship. We are not broken and do not need to be fixed. We definitely do not need those listening to smooth over our areas of weakness by saying "Oh, it wasn't that bad. You did fine." We just need them to listen and affirm that we have been heard. We need them to walk the grief journey with us.

Details

You have probably found yourself sharing in great detail the circumstances surrounding your loved one's death—the illness, the tragedy, what led up to the death, what the last day was like, what the last hour was like, what the last seconds were like, what you did during this time, what happened immediately following the death, who was present, who was not present, the last words your loved one spoke, the words spoken by everyone else in the room, where your loved one is now, and what he is experiencing. Every detail is needed to enable you to come to grips with the reality of your loved one's death and to reconcile it into your own life. There is a good chance that you will tell these details numerous times. That is okay. Your story is precious.

Emotions

Part of your story is how you are feeling. Before you can work through the many emotions on your roller coaster of grief, you have to be aware of the ones you are experiencing. Telling your story is one way for you to identify them, to label them, to normalize their existence, and to walk through each of the emotions. Most grieving individuals have within themselves all they need to work through these emotions and to come to a resolution about them. But we need a "safe" person to help us move forward in this process of discovery.

Fears and Struggles

Many of us have never experienced a loss like this before and walking this uncharted territory is scary. We don't share our fears for the future because we are looking for someone to make them disappear. We are simply looking for someone to listen as we share. We don't share our financial or physical or emotional struggles because we expect our "safe" person to fix them. Rather, we want to be heard. The sharing of our fears and struggles is part of our mourning.

4. Learn What Is Normal in Grief

Having spent years coaching the grieving and hundreds of hours leading grief support groups, there is one question that mourners have asked me far above any other question.

That question is "Am I going crazy?" The second most common question is "Am I normal?"

The journey through grief can be so radically different from our everyday realities that sometimes it feels more like being picked up and dropped onto the surface of the moon than it does a journey through earth. What is unusual in life is often usual in grief. Because we live in a culture that doesn't talk openly about death and grief, most individuals in grief do not know that what they are experiencing is normal. As a matter of fact, they fear just the opposite.

Therefore, one of the greatest and most needed action steps for someone who wants to coach themselves through grief is to learn what is normal. When your coach is with you, she will remind you what is normal in grief. But if you do not have a coach, or in those times when your coach is not present, it will help you to know what's normal in grief.

Every year dozens of people come to me at the suggestion of their doctor. The doctor tells them that they need therapy. Their grief is affecting their everyday behavior and their overall health. They are told they are in need of counseling. Nine times out of ten, these individuals don't need a grief counselor. They need a grief coach to walk alongside of them. They have one primary fact that they need to learn—that what they are experiencing is normal. They are not going crazy. Hearing and understanding those simple words allows them to walk away from my office as a new person. Now, instead of panicking that something is majorly wrong, they feel free to do the work of mourning,

Chapter Three: Grief Coaching Principles

with the support of a coach who will walk the journey of grief with them.

The International Coach Federation lists the "Top Ten Indicators to Refer a Client to a Mental Health Professional." They are as follows:

Your client …

1. Is exhibiting a decline in his/her ability to experience pleasure and/or an increase in being sad, hopeless, and helpless.
2. Has intrusive thoughts or is unable to concentrate or focus.
3. Is unable to get to sleep or awakens during the night and is unable to get back to sleep or sleeps excessively.
4. Has a change in appetite: decrease in appetite or increase in appetite.
5. Is feeling guilty because others have suffered or died.
6. Has feelings of despair or hopelessness.
7. Is being hyper alert and/or excessively tired.
8. Has increased irritability or outbursts of anger.
9. Has impulsive and risk-taking behavior.
10. Has thoughts of death and/or suicide.

Prepared by: Lynn F. Meinke, MA, RN, CLC, CSLC, Life Coach

When the average person exhibits any of these behaviors, especially if they exhibit a number of these behaviors at the same time, it is an indication that they should be referred to a mental health professional. All ten of these behaviors, however, are absolutely normal for someone who is grieving. No wonder the grieving think they are going crazy. Add to this all the extreme emotions that an individual in grief experiences and you can see why one might think they need therapy. Everyone around them who does not understand grief thinks they are in need of therapy, too!

Not only is grief emotional, grief is also physical. In the myths of grief listed earlier, myth #6 was "Grief is only an emotional reaction." Those who buy into this myth and then experience the normal physical symptoms of grief, think they are going crazy.

The reality is that grieving is hard work. It is physically abusive, mentally demanding, and spiritually challenging. I can't think of any other work that I have done that can compare to its intensity or its impact. The exhaustion from grieving is similar to a heavy physical workout.

Below are some common "symptoms" of grieving which are sometimes mistakenly diagnosed as strictly physical problems:

- Chest pains or shortness of breath
- Dizziness or headaches
- Fatigue
- Inability to sleep or sleeping all the time
- Losing sexual desire or drastically increasing sexual desire
- Losing weight or gaining weight

Chapter Three: Grief Coaching Principles

- Increased allergic reactions
- Oversensitivity to noise
- Mindless activity or hyperactivity
- Trembling and weakness
- Uncontrollable sighing and sobbing
- Various gastrointestinal symptoms: dry mouth, "something stuck in the throat," empty feeling in the stomach, nausea, vomiting, constipation, or diarrhea

Any of these symptoms can be a normal part of the grieving process. If they persist or become uncomfortable, you should make an appointment with your health care provider and tell him/her that you have experienced a recent major loss.

Some people find themselves relating to the physical symptoms of the loved one who died, which again makes them think they are going crazy. For example, if their loved one died from a brain tumor, they may have more frequent headaches; if from a heart attack, they may have chest pains. This sometimes becomes an unconscious way of identifying with and feeling close to that person. It is another one of the ways our bodies might respond to our loss.

The grieving individual often does not feel in control of how his body is responding to the stress of grief. This is not a sign of going crazy. In the majority of instances, the physical symptoms described above are normal and temporary.

Concerning their grief, the issue for some people is a spiritual one. "Is it normal for a godly person to grieve?" they ask. "Doesn't the Bible speak down on those who exhibit grief?" When wrestling with this question, reflect on the Scriptures below:

- Blessed are those who mourn, for they shall be comforted (Matthew 5:4).
- The Lord is close to the brokenhearted and saves those who are crushed in spirit (Psalm 34:18).
- The maidens will dance and be glad, young men and old as well. I will turn their mourning into gladness (Jeremiah 31:13).
- God was grieved in his heart (Genesis 6:6).
- Come to me all who are weary and heavy burdened, and I will give you rest (Matthew 11:28 30).

Many who are walking through their grief don't understand all of this. They are exhibiting normal behavior and don't know it! One who desires to coach himself through grief will do well to keep this action step in mind.

5. Take as Much Time As You Need

Today's fast-paced society encourages, and even demands, that we live efficiently. In the proverbial blink of an eye, modern technology makes it possible for us to complete tasks that took previous generations days or weeks. Unfortunately, this has given our generation a "microwave mentality." We want what we want, and we want it now! Look around. There is a fast, quick, instant, speedy service for just about anything we can think of, including espressos, food, medical checkups, and oil changes. Our society has forgotten that quality takes time. We have become impatient. We know the type—the guy who repeatedly punches the elevator call button because it will make the car arrive faster.

Many take this microwave mentality and apply it to the journey of grief. We want it to be quick. We want it done and over with so we can move on with our lives. As I was writing these words, I received a phone call from a man who was part of my Hospice Bereavement Follow Up program. His father died three months ago and, as per practice, I followed up with cards, letters, a monthly newsletter, phone calls, etc. (all produced by the Bereavement Management System—see www.bereavementmanagement.com). This man called to ask that he be removed from the mailing list. His exact words were, "I need to be removed from that list. It's been three months. It is long enough. I would rather not be reminded any more. I would like to just move on." I honored this man's request, but I was concerned about him. The journey of grief cannot be rushed. It is important to remember this when we are tempted to rush through and speed up our grief.

In my experience it's not usually those who are grieving who try to rush the journey; rather, it's those around the grieving who encourage them to do so. People who have not experienced a major loss themselves have a greater chance of buying into the microwave mentality of grief. They expect you to "get over it" quickly. They will push you to do so. One of the most painful, yet oft spoken, phrases to an individual in grief is "Aren't you over it yet?"

You must be aware of this, and you should expect people to say this to you. When they do, don't listen. Give yourself all the time that you need. The pathway of grief is anything but a quick trip. For most people, it is a slow journey which never completely ends. We never forget. (This is a person we have loved. We don't want to forget!) Most of us will continue to grieve for the rest of our lives. Our grief should not continue at the initial intensity. We should learn how to integrate this grief into our lives; yet, it will still be present and, at times, painful.

There is no timetable for getting over grief. There are, however, different time periods in the grief journey that are more difficult than others. You will want to be aware of these.

The First Year

The whole first year of the grief journey is difficult. When your loved one dies, you must not only adjust to your loved one's physical absence, you must experience many "firsts" throughout this year. There will be the first holiday without your loved one; the first birthday without her; the first time you start to call him and realize you can't; the first time you get sick; the first time you go out to dinner alone; the first trip to the craft store without her; the first hunting weekend without him; the first summer or the first winter; etc. Every time you experience one of these "firsts," it is as if your loved one dies all over again. You are hit with a strong wave of the feelings of grief and loss.

It is during this first year, more than any other time, that you will need your grief coach to be walking alongside you in this grief journey. And when your coach is not present, remember these principles of coaching yourself through grief.

There are some specific events during that first year that are typically the most painful:

The First Weeks
The initial weeks following the death of a loved one are, to many, a blur. There is the planning for and the attending of the viewing, the funeral service, and the burial. Greeting all the people who come can be wonderful, yet draining and painful. As difficult as that can be, it only gets worse. The friends and supporters then go home. Life gets back to normal rather quickly for everyone else. For the immediate family, however, the grieving has just started. In addition, for the survivors there is much additional work to be done. Affairs need to be settled quickly and efficiently. At the same time, grief is demanding attention, and the realization is beginning to set in that a deep and permanent change has just been thrust upon you. Those grieving are also beginning to realize that in addition to the primary loss of their loved one, many secondary losses (see chapter four) are being experienced and are complicating their grief.

Three Months
The three-month time period is often difficult for those in grief. The grief and all the emotions that go with it seem to intensify. Those grieving usually have no clue why, but they surely experience it. Often what happens in this time period is that the shock and disbelief and denial are starting to wear off, and you are beginning to face the reality of your loved one's death. Many of your friends and relatives

have moved on and, instead of giving you support, they are now pressuring you to be freed from the pain of what has happened. When you realize you are not "over it," you can sometimes feel shame, wondering what is wrong with you. This adds to the pain and complicates the grief. The emotions are often extreme at this time, and those feelings are absolutely normal. Find your "safe place" to mourn—to let those feelings out, again and again, if that is what it takes.

The Anniversary of the Death
Most people don't need a reminder of the first-year anniversary of their loved one's death. The intensity of grief comes rushing in with a pain that rivals the initial feelings of loss. The anticipation of the anniversary date can be as bad as, if not worse than, the anniversary itself.

My encouragement is that you talk through and plan ahead the way you want to spend the anniversary day. There is nothing worse than waking up on the morning of the anniversary and having no idea how your day will be spent. (Choosing to do nothing that day is fine, as long as that is what you desire, but it should be a conscious decision.) Some people choose to honor their loved one in some way on that day. It might be a day for you to tearfully tell the story of your loved one over again, as you honor the memories and the relationship you and your loved one shared. It might be a day to visit the burial site or a location your loved one liked. Maybe you will choose to make a contribution to a cause she supported. Choose to do (or not do) something meaningful to you.

The anniversary might also be an opportunity for more healing to take place. By reflecting on how you have survived the first year of grief, you may become aware of growth that has taken place in you as you live in the "new normal." Give yourself credit for getting to this point.

Holidays and Special Days
Holidays, birthdays, wedding anniversaries, and other special days can be agonizing for those in grief. Facing these holidays can seem overwhelming. Holidays, more than any other days, can signify "family gatherings." At these times, you might be acutely aware of the void in your life. It is hard to be holly and jolly when your special person is gone. It's hard to gather around the holiday table and see your loved one's chair empty, or filled by the "wrong" person. It is painful to find the perfect gift and to realize your loved one is no longer alive to receive it. All around you, the sounds and sights and smells of the upcoming holiday will trigger memories of your loved one. For some, it is nearly impossible to smile and celebrate a special day when your heart is breaking. Because life as you know it has changed, adjustments need to be made. It can be an opportunity to reassess the way special days are celebrated. Old traditions can be modified and new ones established. There is a lot you might want to talk through in preparation for upcoming holidays and special days.

Articles and entire books are written on this subject. They can provide helpful insights and suggestions for surviving those days, but you will want to be aware of the possible difficulties that they can bring.

Unlike the pretty scenes on our current Christmas cards, the first Christmas was messy and painful. Think of the confused teenaged mom who birthed her first child far from home, perhaps next to noisy animals in a smelly barn. Think of the Father who loves people so much that he gave His only Son over to poverty, pain, danger, and death. Remember that not everyone was thrilled to learn of the coming of the long-awaited Messiah. Feeling threatened, Herod ordered a massacre of all baby boys. If you listened carefully to the sounds throughout the land, you could hear soldiers' threats, babies' cries, and young mothers wailing in desperation. Grief was present everywhere.

6. Don't Let Anyone Tell You What to Do

Although there are aspects of grief that are similar across the board, the reality is that your grief experience is unique. Everyone grieves, but no one else has experienced the exact same things that you are experiencing. Your journey of grief is just that—it is YOUR journey. You as a person are different than anyone else. Your loved one who died was unique. The relationship that the two of you shared, as well as the circumstances that surround the death, are different and unique. Therefore, no two grief experiences are exactly the same.

Alan Wolfelt describes 12 areas of uniqueness that make each one's journey different. He calls them the "whys" of your grief journey (Wolfelt 2003, 35-46):

Why #1: Your relationship with the person who died was different than that person's relationship with anyone else.

Chapter Three: Grief Coaching Principles

The stronger your attachment to the person who died, the more difficult your grief journey will be.

Why #2: The circumstances of the death. How, why, and when the person died can have a definite impact on your grief journey.

Why #3: Decisions you make relating to the ritual or funeral experience can either help or hinder your grief journey.

Why #4: The people that you have or do not have in your life to support you along your journey will make a big difference.

Why #5: Your unique personality will be reflected in your grief.

Why #6: The unique personality of your loved one who died, as well as the role they played in your life, will make a difference.

Why #7: Your gender will affect the way that you grieve, as well as the way others respond to you in your grief.

Why #8: Your cultural background is an important part of how you experience and express your grief.

Why #9: Your religious or spiritual background will have a tremendous impact on your grief journey.

Why #10: Other crises or stresses in your life that you must face at the same time as your loss will affect your experience of grief.

Why #11: Your experiences of loss and death in the past will make a difference.

Why #12: Your physical health has a significant effect on your grief.

YOU are the expert on YOUR grief journey. Nonetheless, you will probably experience many individuals who act as if THEY are the experts on your grief journey. They will tell you that you must do something or act in a certain way, because that is what worked for them. Listen, in case what they have to say is helpful, but do not let them tell you what to do. You are the expert concerning what you need, not them.

Allow me to take this a step further. It is important to remember that even when you have a coach to walk your grief journey with you, they are not the expert—you are. Even if they are a certified end-of-life coach from the coachingatendoflife.com website, YOU are still the expert when it comes to your grief experience.

A second way that we sometimes allow people to tell us what to do is when we compare our grief journey to someone else's. We notice Mary has "moved on" and think, therefore, that we are wrong to still be crying a lot and to still be deep in our mourning. We are told that David still will not leave his house, and so we begin to wonder if perhaps we have started going out to a restaurant to eat too quickly. Your "12 whys" are different than Mary's or David's "12 whys," and therefore your experience is going to be different. Only YOU are the expert as to what you need. Be careful of making comparisons to others.

Chapter Three: Grief Coaching Principles

7. Discover Your New Normal

"Aren't you over it yet?" "Isn't it time you stop crying and get back to normal?"

Many equate grief with having a cold or the flu. You are sick for a time, but then you get over it and are back to normal again. Unfortunately, that is not the way grief works. A far better illustration of what grief is like is that of someone who has just had their leg amputated. The leg is permanently gone. It will never come back. Because of this amputation, this person's life from here on will be forever affected. With a lot of hard work, the amputee can hopefully live a full life again. He can get a prosthesis and learn anew how to walk. Yet, he will forever walk with a limp. He will never forget his "loss." His life will never be the same as it was before his amputation. He will never get back to "normal." He must create a new normal.

Some of the areas where you might be searching for your new normal are:

A New Identity

The loss of your loved one might mean acquiring a new identity. You will never be quite the same as you were before your loved one died. That portion of your life is gone. When someone with whom you have a relationship dies, your self-identity, or the way you see yourself, naturally changes.

Listen to how people introduce themselves. "I am Peter's wife." "I am Helen's son." "I am Linda's sister." "I am Jason's father." When that other person by whom we

45

describe ourselves dies, who are we then? That is something you will need to figure out. You are in search of your new normal. This process (and it is a process—often a long, slow, painful process) is part of forming a new vision for the future.

A New Relationship with the Person Who Died

The goal is not for you to forget your loved one who died. Forming a new identity does not mean disregarding the old one. Rather, the goal is for you to change your relationship with your departed loved one from that of physical presence to that of memory. When a person dies, family and friends are flooded with memories of the deceased—memories of who the person was, things they had done together, funny times they had shared, sad or painful experiences, and lessons that had been learned. So many memories flood the mind of the grieving. I regularly remind those in grief that these memories are precious gifts from God. No one can take them away. The memories are theirs to hold forever. Yet, I encourage those in grief not to hold onto them; rather, I invite them to share the memories with others. I encourage them to keep their loved one alive through the sharing of those memories.

A New Group of Friends

Another aspect of searching for your new normal may include finding new friends with whom you will spend time. If your spouse has died and you as a couple spent most of your time with other couples, chances are you may not feel comfortable with this same group. A widow or widower can feel out of place with a group of married people. Or maybe you spend most of your time socializing with the other families of your child's soccer team. If your child on the soccer team has died, do you still socialize with those other families? Where do you fit in?

You will also find that not everyone is supportive of you in your grief. Dr. Alan D. Wolfelt talks about the rule of thirds (Wolfelt 2003, 127-8). One third of the people in your life will be supportive relationships. They will be "safe" people to share with and will encourage you to do this work of mourning. Another third will turn out to be neutral in your walk of grief. They will neither help nor hinder you in your journey. The final third will be harmful in your effort to mourn well. They will judge you. They will try to get you to stop mourning, and they will not be interested in hearing your story.

A New Sense of Purpose

When someone you love dies, it is normal to question your meaning and purpose in life. You may feel that when your loved one died, a part of you died with him. You wonder what reason there is to go on living.

Perhaps you served as a caregiver for your mother. You got up every day and worked hard to serve her and care for her. You made a difference in her life and knew that she depended on you. You gladly gave your all to meet her needs. Now that she has died, however, what reason do you have to get out of bed? Is there any purpose for your life? Is there any meaning to your current existence?

Whatever your situation, your loss will cause you to search for a new normal. Included in that will be the discovery of a new sense of purpose.

A Renewed Relationship with God

"Why did my loved one die?" "How could God allow this to happen?" These are normal questions when a loved one dies. Some of those in grief draw close to God as a way of seeking help through their loss. Others experience times of doubt and question the very existence of God. Both responses are a means of seeking a new sense of meaning following their loss. This questioning is normal and is all part of searching for a new normal.

Discovering a new normal is not easy, but it is essential in moving forward in grief.

8. Celebrate Your Growth

Walking the journey of grief is life-changing. No one chooses to experience grief. It is almost always unwanted and unplanned. Yet for many, the journey of grief is a wonderful growing experience.

Growth through grief comes in many forms. For some, it is an increased sensitivity toward people who are going through difficulties. For others, it is a better understanding of themselves. They are able to accomplish things they never dreamed possible and move forward in life with increased confidence. Still others come through their grief journey with a commitment to give back what others have given them. They volunteer for hospice, visit their church's shut-ins, or seek out those who are grieving a loss. Some learn to appreciate each moment of each day, learning what a gift life is. They live as fully as possible. Others realize growth in their relationship with God, get involved in their local food bank, commit to serving in their local hospital, or raise funds for the Relay for Life. The possibilities are endless.

The eighth action step is for you to recognize this growth. Note: this does not occur right away. You might even be angry reading this eighth action step. You cannot imagine growth or anything good ever coming out of your loss. That is okay. Those feelings are normal and quite common early on. Be honest about those feelings right now. But be aware that, much later, many people realize there are things they learned along the way. Although they wish their loved one had never died, they admit that their grief has made them a better person.

When you do come to that place, don't forget to celebrate your growth.

Chapter Four
Dealing with the Losses of Life

Throughout this book, my focus has been on individuals whose loved one has died. The principles learned here, however, are applicable to those who are dealing with all the losses of life.

Loss is one of our constant companions throughout life. For many, LOSS is truly a four-letter word—it is a curse word, not to be mentioned. But for most of us, it is almost always there. Each one of us faces issues of loss all the time.

From the moment we are conceived, our lives are a series of transitions:

- We slide from the dark, cozy womb into the bright, cold world—a shocking transition, indeed.
- We nurse at the breast and then we are weaned.
- We attach to our parents, then are forced to detach from them when we are placed in day care or preschool.
- Our baby teeth fall out.
- We make friends and lose them.

- Our parents may divorce.
- We sometimes move to a new neighborhood.
- We leave home to go to school.
- A pet dies.
- A best friend moves away.
- A boyfriend or girlfriend decides they no longer love us.
- We get a job, and we lose it.
- A person we love dies.
- We learn we are dying.

(Adapted from *Living in the Shadow of the Ghosts of Grief*, Wolfelt 2007, pp. 13-14.)

We could go on and on. Life is filled with transitions and losses.

Nobody likes to lose. Life is supposed to be filled with winners. Look at the headlines on the sports pages.

Losing hurts. It causes pain. It hurts even more because we haven't been taught to expect loss as a part of life, nor have we been taught how to handle the losses of life.

We want to be winners. We want success. We want to be in control of our lives, so we build walls around us with signs that say, "Losses—No Trespassing!" Then, when they occur, we feel violated. We say something is wrong. We get angry with God. But the problem is that they keep occurring. We can't get away from them.

Chapter Four: Dealing with the Losses of Life

We have good reason to dislike loss. Too often, a person who has suffered a loss is blamed for it:

- If she were a better wife, he would have stayed.
- They failed as parents. Otherwise, that child wouldn't have become involved with that crowd.
- He lost his job. I wonder what he did wrong.
- No wonder he got cancer. He should have taken better care of himself.

People in Jesus' day had the same thoughts. In John 9:1-3, we're told:

> As Jesus went along, he saw a man blind from birth. His disciples asked him, "Rabbi, who sinned, this man or his parents, that he was born blind?" "Neither this man nor his parents sinned," said Jesus, "but this happened so that the works of God might be displayed in him.

Losses are a part of life. Ecclesiastes 3:1-4 states:

> There is a time for everything, and a season for every activity under the heavens: a time to be born and a time to die, a time to plant and a time to uproot, a time to kill and a time to heal, a time to tear down and a time to build, a time to weep and a time to laugh, a time to mourn and a time to dance.

Not only are losses a part of life, but losses come in all shapes and sizes.

Coach Yourself Through Grief

Some losses are over in 24 hours. Others last for years. Others you never get over. How you respond to your losses, or what you let them do to you, will affect you the rest of your life. You can't avoid loss or shrug it off. Loss is going to be a part of our lives, whether we acknowledge those losses or not.

Loss is not the enemy; not facing its existence is. Unfortunately, many of us have become more proficient in developing denial than we are in facing and accepting the losses of life.

Truthfully, loss isn't always bad. As a matter of fact, loss can be good! With each loss comes the potential for change, growth, new insights, understanding, and refinement—all words of hope. The problem is that they are often in the future, and we are unable to see that far ahead when we are in the midst of our grief.

Life is a blending of loss and gain. Let me give you some examples:

- A bud is lost when it turns into a beautiful rose.
- When a plant pushes its way up through the soil, a seed is lost.
- When you were a child, your baby teeth came in after bouts of pain and crying, but they were lost in order to make room for the permanent teeth. Sometimes these too are lost and replaced by false teeth.
- Graduating from high school produced a loss of status, friends, and familiarity, but most of us looked forward to it, for it meant getting on with our lives.

Chapter Four: Dealing with the Losses of Life

Change usually involves some form of loss of the way things were at one time.

In the New Testament, the Apostle Paul told the Ephesians (4:22-24):

> You were taught, with regard to your former way of life, to put off your old self ... and to put on the new self. ... The 'new self' comes as a result of the loss of the 'old self.'

Some of the losses of life can be obvious: losing a loved one through death or divorce, a car is stolen, or a house is vandalized.

Some are not as obvious: changing jobs, receiving a "B" instead of an "A" in a college course, getting less than we had hoped for in a raise, moving, illness (loss of health), a new teacher in the middle of a semester, a son or daughter going off to school, or the loss of a dream or lifetime goal. All of these are losses, but because they may not be easy to recognize, we do not identify them as such. Therefore, we don't spend time and energy dealing with them.

Many of the losses of life are related to aging.

Childhood and adolescent romances are filled with losses—some daily, even hourly! Moving from school to school, failing a grade, dropping out, leaving home for college, or moving away from family, even if planned—these changes contain loss.

When we hit the job market, losses multiply as rejections occur: someone else gets the promotion, deals fall through, businesses fail, or the economy falters.

There are physical losses—ironically, a major one involves the gain of pounds and inches! We lose our youth beauty, smooth skin, muscle tone, or our shape.

In the middle years, the losses become more frequent and more negative. Who rejoices over lost hair, lost teeth, or graduating to bifocals? We don't usually call these growth experiences. Losses seem to build on losses. We tend to lose more friends as the years go on.

Threatened losses are difficult. The possibility of their occurrence is real, but there is little you can do about it. Your sense of control is destroyed. You've been working for 19 years at the same company. At 20 years, all of your benefits are secure. Then you are informed that, due to a sluggish economy, 40 percent of the employees at your company will be terminated at the end of the month, and length of employment is no criteria for being retained. Will you be one of the 40 percent?

There are many other threatened losses in life: waiting for biopsy results; a spouse who says, "I'm thinking of divorcing you"; a romantic interest who doesn't call anymore; a business investment that may not come through; being sued by an angry customer or employee; or a friend who tells you he suspects your son has been using drugs for the past year.

All of the above are potential losses. They could occur. There is little you can do about them, and you feel the loss before it occurs—you feel helpless.

Chapter Four: Dealing with the Losses of Life

Being part of a church or parish or synagogue brings losses that would not be there otherwise. People leave the church. Sometimes clergy leave. Sometimes there are church splits.

There are losses that come as a result of divorce. There are losses that come as a result of abandonment—whether physical or emotional abandonment.

Having a disease such as cancer is considered a major loss because of the health change. But have you considered all the additional secondary losses? These include loss of a familiar home environment, loss of independence, loss of control, loss of bodily functions, loss of body parts, loss of predictability, loss of pleasure, loss of identity, loss of intimacy, loss of hope, loss of job, loss of enjoyable hobbies, loss of social interaction or contacts, loss of self-esteem, or loss of mobility.

The death of a significant person is what we usually think of first when we talk about grief or loss, but how about all the secondary losses that go along with that—loss of hopes, dreams, and the needs you had for that person. It's not only what you lose in the present, but what you lose in the future as well.

A widow has not only lost her husband, but has also lost a partner to share retirement, couples' groups, a child's wedding, a grandchild's first birthday, and so on. A son has not only lost his father, he's also lost his sports buddy, hunting partner, etc. A woman has not only lost her sister, she's lost her only true confidant, or her children's favorite babysitter.

Identifying some of the roles that a deceased person played in your life may help you understand the direction your life will now be taking. As you think about your loss, consider which of the following apply:

Friend	Child
Handyperson	Parent
Lover	Brother
Gardener	Sister
Companion	Provider
Sports partner	Cook
Checkbook balancer	Bill payer
Garbage taker-outer	Laundry person
Mechanic	Confidant
Encourager	Mentor
Motivator	Prayer partner
Business partner	Source of inspiration
Errand person	Teacher
Tax preparer	Counselor
Spouse	Protector

Understand?

These are all common losses. The majority of losses we experience are difficult to grieve. Why? Because they are not usually recognized as losses. The trouble with trying to mourn loss when death isn't involved is that there is no body, no funeral, and no public shoulder to cry on. There is no traditional, socially sanctioned outlet for mourning when the loss isn't death (Wright, *Recovering from Losses in Life*, 2006, 19).

Chapter Four: Dealing with the Losses of Life

And, you see, losses are cumulative. Past losses have an effect on current losses and attachments. When we don't deal with the losses of life—when we don't properly grieve them—unresolved reactions and feelings lead to a higher level of discomfort. These unresolved issues continue to prevent us from living life to the fullest. There are times when we lose hope and remain stuck with pain from the past.

Have you ever caught some flies and imprisoned them in a glass jar with air holes at the top? Some of us did this as children. If you do this, you will notice that the flies buzz around frantically looking for a way out of the jar. But keep the jar closed for several days and something interesting begins to happen. When you take the perforated lid off, the flies don't try to escape. Even though there is no lid, the flies are so used to flying around in a circle, they continue to do so. Even when they get close to the top, they go right back to flying around in a circle.

Well, sometimes people do the same thing. We carry our losses with us like emotional baggage. Even though the lid of the jar has been removed, we continue to fly in circles.

Who taught you how to handle the losses of life? For most of us, probably no one did. In our families, we are taught that acquisition of things, whether material or nonmaterial, is the way to be happy and satisfied. We learn to be good in order to receive attention and praise from parents and other adults. In school, the acquisition of grades gives acceptance and approval. Parents rarely teach us how to handle loss, disappointment, and failure.

The drive to acquire continues throughout life. Isn't that what advertisers tell us is needed to be successful? Thus, we grow up with the myth that "acquiring is normal; loss is abnormal." Loss to us feels wrong and unnatural. How you respond to losses today and tomorrow may be the result of how you responded to the early losses in your life.

Every loss is important. It is part of life and cannot be avoided. You grow by losing and then accepting the loss. Change occurs through loss. Growth occurs through loss. Life can take on a deeper and richer meaning because of losses. The better you handle them, the healthier you will be and the more you will grow. No one said that loss was fair, but it is a part of life.

For people of faith, the issue of loss has additional meaning—spiritual growth. Loss can strengthen our faith. It enables us to trust more in God and His resources than in ourselves. With every loss, we are reminded of the fact that we are not in control, and we are not self-sufficient. Loss produces maturity. Romans 5:3-4 says:

> Not only so, but we also glory in our sufferings, because we know that suffering produces perseverance; perseverance, character; and character, hope.

Loss reminds us that we cannot always have immediate gratification. We can't always have what we want, when we want it, no matter what.

When you experience a loss, like the Apostle Paul, your beliefs can change. Paul discovered the purpose of losses.

Chapter Four: Dealing with the Losses of Life

In 2 Corinthians 12:1-10, he talked about his thorn in the flesh. He wanted it to leave and it wouldn't. But he learned that there was a purpose for this thorn. God's power would be more evident in his life because of its presence.

When you experience loss, you might discover the extent of the comfort of God. 2 Corinthians 1:3 states:

> Praise be to the God and Father of our Lord Jesus Christ, the Father of compassion and the God of all comfort, who comforts us in all our troubles, so that we can comfort those in any trouble with the comfort we ourselves receive from God.

Loss can bring people together in a way never experienced before. We are called to comfort each other (1 Thess. 4:18) and to weep with those who weep (Rom. 12:15).

Our losses can change our values. The questions "Why did I spend so much time on that?" and "Why did I waste all those years?" are common when one is grieving over the loss of a loved one. Hopefully, we will learn through those experiences so that we can make changes in our lives.

The key to all of this is: Our losses must be dealt with! We need to be aware of them! We need to grieve them! As Alan Wolfelt (2007) states, "If you want to live well and love well, you need to mourn well."

Hopefully, you are learning how to do just that.

Chapter Five
Our Culture's View of Grief

We live in a culture that does not deal well with end-of-life issues. Many don't want to face the reality of death. People don't even like to talk about death. For many, the subject is taboo. If the topic arises, some will change the subject. Others will walk away. For some people, the underlying assumption is that, if I talk about death, it might happen to me. So, I am not going to even mention it.

As a result of this underlying assumption, we have come up with many euphemisms related to dying and death. There are literally hundreds of euphemisms for death in the English language. Instead of saying someone has died, we say they expired, passed away, or kicked the bucket. They bit the big one, croaked, or have given up the ghost. We refer to a dead person as being six feet under, or say they are pushing up daisies. We say they cashed in their chips or checked out. They danced the last dance and have bought the farm. All this and much, much more, simply because we don't like to mention the word "dead."

While some purposely don't talk about end-of-life issues, I get the sense that for others, we have been so conditioned by our culture that we fail to accept that death is inevitable. Many of us act as if death is optional.

Think about it. There are many physicians that seldom discuss life's final stage. They continue to offer treatments to their patients, even when they are of little or no benefit.

When a person has a loved one who dies, they are faced with the reality of death. Yet those around them may still refuse to acknowledge this reality. The mourner has to be back to work in three days or less. Some will never mention a word about his or her loss. Others will make comments such as, "It's been a month. Aren't you over it yet?" In other words, they are saying, "You are making me uncomfortable! Please don't talk about it! Please don't make me face this reality!"

It would be so much easier if we could turn to our families, our friends, or our workplaces to find the support we need in working through our grief. (That is part of the vision of Coaching at End of Life.) Unfortunately, right now that is not the reality. Many people in grief must coach themselves through grief and/or partner with a certified end-of-life coach for a period of time.

Chapter Six

The Church: Help or Hindrance?

So ... how about the church?

When a loved one has died and the survivors are grieving, is the church a place where they can turn to find help? Can they find people who will walk the journey of grief with them? Is this not the place to turn to find the Lord's help?

The answer to each of those questions should be YES! There should be no greater or more helpful place to find help or companionship when dealing with end-of-life issues. This is the place where the answers should be found! However, my experience shows that what "should" be is not always the case. As a matter of fact, I would go so far as to say that more often than not, I see and hear stories of the church being more of a hindrance than a help to those who are grieving. It saddens me greatly, because it need not be that way. I pray that in time this will change. This is my vision and it is my prayer.

How can the church end up being more of a hindrance than a help? Consider some thoughts:

Cultural Principles Permeate the Church

In the last chapter, we talked about the culture in which we live. It is a culture that does not want to deal with end-of-life issues. Many don't like to talk about it. They avoid the topic at any cost and, in the process, avoid the individuals who are in the midst of an end-of-life crisis.

Since the church is made up of people—people who are part of the current culture—it becomes easy for those same feelings and responses to become part of the church. Those who are grieving the loss of a loved one will sometimes feel just as isolated and alone as those who are not a part of a church. Why? Often the church culture is not any different. In many cases, it is even more difficult for churchgoers, because they expect it to be different. They expect their church family to support them and are devastated when they don't.

The Clergy Don't Know Any Better

It is not only the parishioners who bring into the church our current cultural ideas concerning end-of-life issues. The clergy often do the same. It's not a conscious choice. Rather, they were never taught how to guide people through grief and loss.

I think back to my own story. I had a wonderful seminary experience. I felt well-prepared for pastoral ministry. I remember one lecture in my Pastoral Counseling class dealing with grief and loss, and I remember one class in my Preaching Course dealing with funerals. That, however,

Chapter Six: The Church: Help or Hindrance

was the extent of my training on end-of-life issues. I am not blaming my seminary. There is only so much material that can fit into a three-year program. I am just trying to point out the reality. What made all of this worse is that I had no clue how little I knew. I thought I was prepared to minister to people who were dealing with end-of-life issues. Yet I look back now on my early years of ministry, and I realize that in many cases I was more of a hindrance than a help. That makes me sad. My own inadequacies were contributing factors to the founding of Coaching at End of Life. My own story has made me passionate about helping other clergy learn to minister in end-of-life issues.

Another major issue for clergy is lack of time. Clergy are stretched thin and simply do not have the time to give extensive care. Bereaved parishioners feel isolated as the pastor moves on to the next family crisis. (Parishioners who want to see a change in their church in regard to this issue are encouraged to recommend Bereavement Management System software as a solution. See www.bereavementmanagement.com for more information.)

Typical Godly Response

When you take a group from a faith community and add to that group other people whose primary training on end-of-life issues is from our current culture, you get the following:

When it comes to caring for the grieving, the problem I typically see in the church is that the members and clergy care too much. They are too nice! How can one care too much or be too nice? When a person experiences a loss, the most important thing for them to do is to mourn that loss. The church becomes a hindrance when they care so much about making the individual feel comfortable that they don't allow them to mourn. They don't want their friend or parishioner to hurt or feel bad. This is admirable, but it doesn't allow the grieving to grieve.

Fear

Sometimes the issue is fear:

- I am afraid they will ask me something I cannot do or cannot answer.
- I am afraid of what to say. I don't want to make it worse.
- I don't want to evoke strong feelings.
- I was taught how to do, not how to be or what to say to individuals and families who are dealing with end-of-life issues.
- If I ask an open-ended question, I don't know where the conversation will go. I am afraid to make them cry.
- I am afraid it will make me cry. I am so sensitive.

Misuse of Scripture or Bad Theology

To say that Christians ought not to grieve is ridiculous. This is cruel and amounts to telling them to "get over it." Yet well-meaning people (clergy and non-clergy alike) convey these sentiments over and over again: "If you mourn, shed tears, get scared, show excessive emotions, or question 'why,' you are showing a lack of faith and are not trusting God. That's what the Bible says!" Whether similar words are spoken or

Chapter Six: The Church: Help or Hindrance

just implied by people's behaviors, I understand why some people avoid going to church while in the midst of grief. They find churches to be a hindrance rather than a help.

The Bible states, "We don't want you to ... grieve like the rest of men, who have no hope" (1 Thess. 4:13). Experiencing grief and mourning your loss are in no way a sign of being a person who lacks faith. The Apostle Paul does say that we should not grieve as those who have no hope—but he never says "Don't grieve!" Paul is expressing that true, godly grief, as real as it is, should be tempered by the unshakable hope grounded in the resurrection of the Savior, Jesus Christ.

The grieving experience a whole range of emotions that are normal. Look to the Old Testament to see how Job experienced and worked through his spectrum of emotions. He was numb as he encountered one loss after another, losing everything that he considered precious. He was angry when his wife told him to curse God and die. He was probably frightened as his illnesses continued to worsen. He was upset that he could not seem to die. He was at first glad and then sad when his three friends showed up to comfort him, and as they continued to "comfort" him, he grew increasingly lonely because they proved to be no comfort at all. He wanted them to leave! That is all normal grief—not an expression of a lack of faith.

Acts 8:2 says, "Godly men buried Stephen and mourned deeply for him." This fits right into the Apostle Paul's directive to the Romans to "mourn with those who mourn" (Romans 2:15). The elders of the Ephesian church reacted in this way when Paul left them: "They all wept ... What grieved them most was his statement that they would never see his face again" (Acts 20:37-38).

Scripture has numerous examples of intense grief. Abraham and Isaac mourned the loss of Sarah (Gen. 23:2; 24:67). The Israelites grieved the death of Jacob (Gen. 50:10), Aaron (Num. 20:29), Moses (Deut. 34:8), Samuel (1 Sam. 28:3), Saul and Jonathan (2 Sam. 1:12, 17), and Josiah (2 Chron. 35:25), along with many others. In the New Testament, Jesus withdrew privately to grieve the death of John the Baptist (Matt. 14:13). He openly wept in grief and in empathy with his friends Mary and Martha at the tomb of their brother Lazarus (John 11:35). Devout believers mourned the death of the deacon Stephen (Acts 8:2). Godly women wept openly for the loss of Tabitha in Joppa (Acts 9:39).

All this, yet some well-meaning pastors and church members say it is inappropriate to grieve openly, and that it shows a lack of faith. No wonder some who are grieving stay away from the church, saying it is more of a hindrance than a help!

The Use of Clichés—Religious & Secular

Many people are uncomfortable with silence and, when they talk with someone facing end-of-life issues, they feel the need to say something. As I spend time listening to the grieving, one of the biggest frustrations I hear concerns the comments that others make to them. Not knowing what to say, the "consolers" frequently put their foot in their mouth and say things that are hurtful or harmful to the one they are trying to console. The church is no exception to this. As

Chapter Six: The Church: Help or Hindrance

a matter of fact, it is one of the most common places where people are faced with these clichés. Sadly, the religious clichés are the most devastating. There is no easy way to respond to them.

This is such a common frustration and a major hindrance to the help and healing of the grieving, an entire book could be written on just this topic! For the sake of brevity, however, allow me to share some of the most popular clichés I hear—both religious and secular—which hinder those in grief:

- Death happens. Get over it.
- Life goes on.
- Count your blessings.
- It was God's will.
- You are still young. You can have another child/marry again.
- There are other fish in the sea.
- God only takes the best and the brightest.
- Be grateful you had him for as long as you did.
- He's in a better place now.
- Something must have been wrong already.
- You are better off.
- Keep your chin up.
- God doesn't give you anything you can't handle.
- Be thankful you have another daughter.
- You have to get on with your life.

- There is a reason for everything.
- You have your whole life ahead of you.
- Just think of all you have to be thankful for.
- I know how you feel.
- You should be glad he/she is out of pain.
- There are other people in much worse situations.
- Time will heal.
- She was so good, God wanted her with Him.
- God called you to this ministry.
- At least you didn't have time to get attached to your baby.
- She brought this on herself.
- Try not to cry. He/she wouldn't want you to cry.
- It's time to put this behind you.
- Aren't you over him yet? He has been dead for a while now.
- It could have been worse.
- If you think this is bad, I know a family …
- This isn't nearly as bad as when my mother died.
- It must be a relief.

The Need to Defend God

I will mention here one final reason that the church can end up being more of a hindrance than a help when it comes to end-of-life issues. It's when religious people feel the need to defend God.

Chapter Six: The Church: Help or Hindrance

Facing end-of-life issues is never fun. It is almost never one's choice to go through it. As a matter of fact, most people pray that they will be spared from going through it! The problem comes when this prayer is not answered, or at least not answered the way they want.

Following the death of a loved one, the most often asked question is "Why?" "Why did God take my loved one?" "Why didn't He answer my prayer and heal him?"

Many get angry at God. "How could a loving God do this?"

Some wonder if God is punishing them for some sin they have committed. They are upset because God has rejected them, and they don't understand why.

Some will curse God!

All of the above are normal reactions following the death of a loved one. The anger is expressed toward God. Telling these people that they are out of line with their comments, or trying to defend God is not the most helpful response. For one, God does not need to be defended. But even more, standing up for God is not what will help draw the hurting individual closer to God (which is usually the church member's intent). When the church feels the need to defend God in these situations, the result is usually to push the person away from God. Those who defend God to the grieving end up being far more of a hindrance than a help.

Chapter Seven
Finding an End-of-Life Coach

How does one go about finding an end-of-life coach with whom to walk the journey of grief?

The easiest way is to go to the coachingatendoflife.com website and look under the list of certified end-of-life coaches listed there. Each individual listed has completed the Coaching at End of Life training and has been tested and certified in their end of life coaching skills. Read the profiles and find one that sounds like a good match to you. Most will offer a free end of life coaching session, so you can find one compatible with your particular needs. Contact me or any of the certified coaches with any questions you might have.

If you are looking for a friend to walk the grief journey with you, find someone "safe" with whom you can be yourself and can share anything. You might even want to give him a copy of this book, asking him to read it before you elicit his support. Tell him this is the grief model you would like to follow and see if he will support you in it.

If at any time your coach tries to fix you or tell you what to do or acts like the expert, talk to him about it. If necessary, seek a new coach—one who will treat you as the expert you are and who will walk your journey with you. Having the right coach is too important to settle for anything less than what you really need.

Chapter Eight
Grief Support Groups

In addition to having your own coach, many find help in attending grief support groups. There are four primary purposes that are accomplished in grief support groups. First of all, grief support groups remind the one in grief that he is not alone. To be in the presence of others who are experiencing similar thoughts and feelings can prove invaluable.

Secondly, grief support groups remind one in grief that she is normal and is not going crazy, as she might have initially feared. Seeing others experience some of the same "crazy" things that she is experiencing can help her say, "If all these other individuals are experiencing some of the same stuff I am, then maybe I am okay."

Thirdly, grief support groups become a place for many to be instructed on what is normal in grief and to learn what it means to mourn a loss. As stated earlier, this is not something we learn in our culture. Grief instruction is a necessity for many.

Fourthly, grief support groups become a social outlet for many people. They are grateful to be connected to other people who "get" what they are going through. Often deep, lasting friendships and relationships are formed through grief support groups.

There are a variety of types of grief support groups that meet. Some are faith based groups. Some are specific for certain groups—teenagers who lost a parent; loss of a spouse, or child; or people who have had a loved one die by suicide, or by cancer, or in a tragic accident. Some are short-term groups—seven weekly sessions and then they disband. Other groups are ongoing, for example, meeting monthly with no end date.

There are various means by which one can be involved in a grief support group. The traditional method is to meet at a common location and to support one another in person. For those who are not able to get out, or are not ready to face people, some support groups meet over the telephone. Still others prefer to "type" rather than "talk." Online grief support groups via a chat room provide that perfect opportunity. (See coachingatendoflife.com for some telephone groups you might want to join or for information on how you can participate in an online support group.)

In addition to the coachingatendoflife.com website, some of the places where you can locate available grief support groups are:

- Google "grief support groups in (town, state)."
- Check with local hospice organizations.

- Check with your local hospital.
- Many churches/faith-based organizations provide grief support groups that are open to the community.
- Ask your doctor.
- Look in the community section of your newspaper.

Most grief support groups will specify certain "ground rules" by which they operate. You will want to make sure that these group rules are in keeping with the coaching model of grief support listed in this book. As a sample of what you might be looking for, below are the ground rules I follow in my groups:

1. Each person's grief is unique. While you may share some commonalities in your experiences, no two of you are exactly alike. Consequently, respect and accept both what you share in common with others in the group and what is unique to you.

2. Grief is not a disease. No "quick-fix" exists for what you are feeling. Healing is a process, not an event. Don't set a specific timetable for how long it takes you or others to heal.

3. Feel free to talk about your grief. However, if someone in the group decides to listen without sharing, please respect his or her preference.

4. A difference exists between actively listening to what another person is saying and expressing your own grief. Make every effort not to interrupt when someone else is speaking.

5. Thoughts, feelings, and experiences shared in this group will stay in this group. Respect others' right to confidentiality. Do not use the names of fellow participants in discussions outside of the group.

6. Allow each person equal time to express himself or herself, so a few people can't monopolize the group's time.

7. Attend the group meetings for as long as you desire. There is no set time when you must stop coming. Please do your best to arrive on time, and we will be sure to end the group on time.

8. Avoid "advice giving" unless it is specifically requested by a group member. If advice is not solicited, don't give it. If a group member poses a question, share ideas that helped you if you experienced a similar situation whenever possible. This group is for support, not therapy.

9. Recognize that thoughts and feelings are neither right nor wrong. Enter into the thoughts and feelings of other group members without trying to change them.

10. Create an atmosphere of willing, invited sharing. If you feel pressured to talk but don't want to, say so. Your right to quiet contemplation will be respected by the group.

Chapter Nine
Anytime Grief Support

I hear over and over again, "I would never be where I am if it were not for my group."

The problem with grief support groups, however, is that they only meet monthly or weekly at best. That is a problem because grief, as we all know, knows no schedule or timetable. Most of us experience bursts of grief at various times of the day and night, sometimes when we least expect it or want it.

Because our coach is not with us 24/7, we said it is important to learn how to coach ourselves through grief. In a similar way, there needs to be an alternative to our regularly scheduled grief support groups. That alternative is the anytime grief support found on the coachingatendoflife.com webpage.

Here, at any time of the day or night, you can sign online and blog about what you are feeling or experiencing. If others happen to be online at the same time, you can invite them to chat with you. You may want to post pictures of your loved one or write about her apple pies, or describe his sense of humor, or … You get the idea. You'll have a way to honor your loved one, as well as give and receive support at any time.

Chapter Ten

How Do I Become an End-of-Life Coach?

After having a certified end-of-life coach walk the grief journey with them, some people decide they would like to do the same for others. (This is part of their "growth" that takes place, as described in action step 8 in Chapter Three of this book.) I receive regular inquiries about how one can be educated and equipped to become a certified end-of-life coach.

See the coachingatendoflife.com website. The calendar lists open onsite and online trainings. Contact me if you want to host an onsite training near you.

Participants use the textbook "Coaching at End of Life," available on the coachingatendoflife.com website.

I would love to discuss any of these options with you. We live in a world that is hurting. There are many trying to work through their grief on their own, desperately in need of a coach to walk with them. Maybe you are part of their answer.

Dr. Don Eisenhauer
Coaching at End of Life
don@coachingatendoflife.com
484-948-1894

Resources

Principles for Coaching Yourself Through Grief

1. Find a Safe Place
2. Board the Roller Coaster and Hold on Tight
3. Tell Your Story
4. Learn what is Normal in Grief
5. Take as Much Time as You Need
6. Don't Let Anyone Tell You What to Do
7. Discover Your New Normal
8. Celebrate Your Growth

Download the Coaching at End of Life App

Search "Coaching at End of Life" in your Apple or Google Store to download this free App.

From this App you can access the Coaching at End of Life website, find a certified end-of-life coach to walk your grief journey with you, locate grief support groups, access the Anytime Grief Support opportunities, and receive notifications of upcoming news and events.

Free eBook: Life Lessons from Dragonflies

How do you feel about dragonflies?

If you saw a dragonfly near you, would you allow it to land on your arm? Would you be scared to do so? Why are they called dragonflies? They don't look like dragons! And what is it with their eyes? They're so big!

Have you given much thought to what dragonflies can teach you? (No, I'm not joking!)

I am not alone in my fascination with dragonflies. Dragonfly symbolism plays a role in many cultures in the world. In different times and places, the dragonfly has been associated with both good and evil.

Learn more about what the dragonfly can teach us about life, and how it can help us face the inevitable end of life issues. To get your free ebook, fill out the form at http://coachingatendoflife.com/free-e-book-life-lessons-from-dragonflies.

Life Lessons From Dragonflies

Helping us face the inevitable end of life issues

By Dr. Don Eisenhauer, PCC

References

Eisenhauer, Don. *Coaching at End of Life: A Coach Approach to Ministering to the Dying and the Grieving.* Coaching4Clergy, 2012.

Eisenhauer, Don. *Life Lessons from Dragonflies: Helping us face the inevitable end of life issues.* PDF Edition. 2012.

International Coach Federation. "Top Ten Indicators to Refer a Client to a Mental Health Professional," prepared by Meinke, Lynn F., MA, RN, CLC, CSLC. http://www.coachfederation.org. 2007.

Kubler-Ross, Elizabeth. *On Death and Dying.* London: Routledge, 1973.

NIV Pastor's Bible. Grand Rapids: Zondervan Publishing House, 2000.

Wolfelt, Alan D. *Living in the Shadow of the Ghosts of Grief.* Fort Collins, CO: Companion Press, 2007.

Wolfelt, Alan D. *Understanding Your Grief.* Fort Collins, CO: Companion Press, 2003.

Wright, H. Norman. *Helping Those Who Hurt: Reaching Out to Your Friends in Need.* Bloomington, MN: Bethany House Publishers, 2006.

Wright, H. Norman. *Recovering from Losses in Life.* Grand Rapids, MI: Fleming H. Revell, 2006.

About the Author

Dr. Don Eisenhauer is a pastor and a Professional Certified Coach, accredited by the International Coach Federation. He is the founder and president of Coaching at End of Life, LLC (www.coachingatendoflife.com), providing end of life training, resources, and coach certification. In addition to doing end of life coaching and leading grief support groups, Don serves as a Hospice Chaplain and Bereavement Coordinator. He is also on the faculty of Coaching4Clergy.

Other publications include the eBook *Life Lessons from Dragonflies: Helping us face the inevitable end of life issues,"* and the text book *Coaching at End of Life: A Coach Approach to Ministering to the Dying and the Grieving*, coauthored with J. Val Hastings, MCC. Don has a passion to help people live fully until they die, and to help equip pastors and other church leaders minister to the dying and the grieving. He is also the co-founder of the Bereavement Management Group, providing software to help in the care of the grieving. You can learn more about this program at www.bereavementmanagement.com.

Bereavement Management Group

Printed in Great Britain
by Amazon